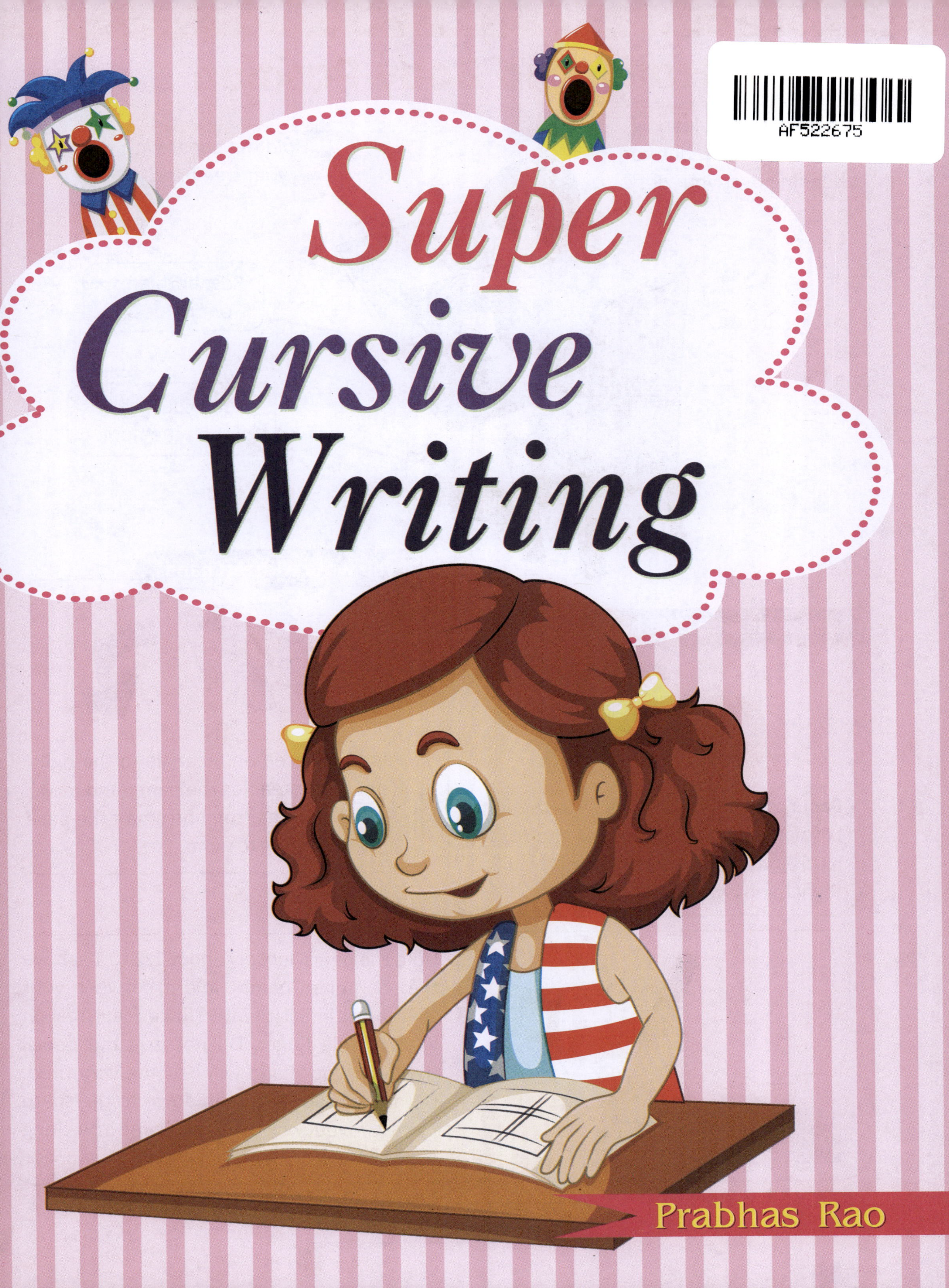

AF522675
Super
Cursive
Writing
Prabhas Rao

Hand and Body Position

If you write with right hand.

Paper is placed on an angle to the left . Lefthand steadies the paper and moves it up as you near the bottom of the page. Right hand is free to write.

If you write with left hand.

Paper is placed on an angle to the right . Right hand steadies the paper and moves it up as you near the bottom of the page. Left hand is free to write.

Hold the pencil loosely about 1/2 to 1" above the sharpened point. Hold it between your thumb and index (pointer) finger. Let it rest on your middle finger. Do not grip the pencil tightly or your hand will become very tired. Do not let your hand slip down to the sharp point or you will have difficulty in writing properly.

orchid sunflower jasmine

orchid sunflower jasmine

orchid sunflower jasmine

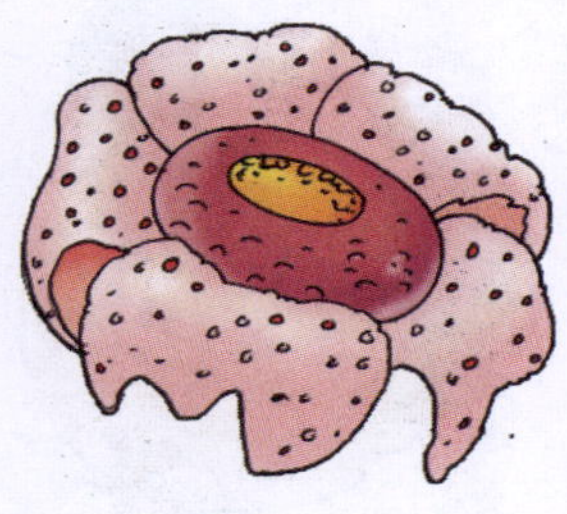

calendula lotus rafflesia

calendula lotus rafflesia

calendula lotus rafflesia

apple avocado banana

apple avocado banana

apple avocado banana

orange mango guava

orange mango guava

orange mango guava

turnip pumpkin radish

turnip pumpkin radish

turnip pumpkin radish

asparagus beetroot tomato

asparagus beetroot tomato

asparagus beetroot tomato

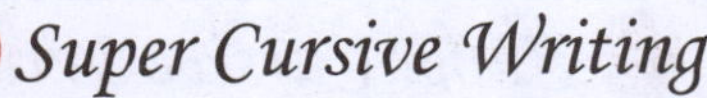

hippo elephant dinosaur

hippo elephant dinosaur

hippo elephant dinosaur

crocodile kangaroo lion

crocodile kangaroo lion

crocodile kangaroo lion

parrot peacock cuckoo

parrot peacock cuckoo

parrot peacock cuckoo

ostrich kingfisher eagle

ostrich kingfisher eagle

ostrich kingfisher eagle

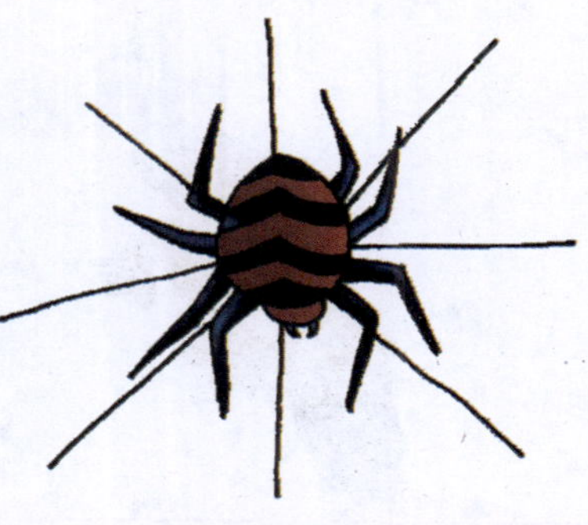

cockroach spider scorpion

cockroach spider scorpion

cockroach spider scorpion

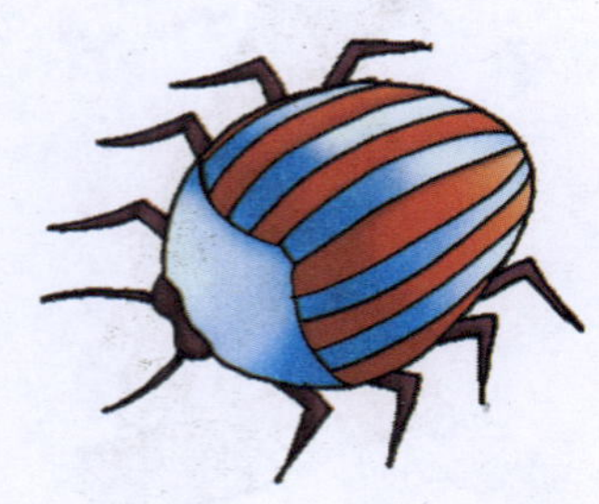

bettle termite mosquito

bettle termite mosquito

bettle termite mosquito

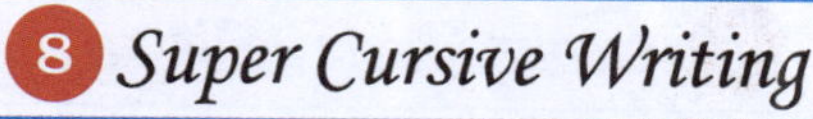

Animal's sounds

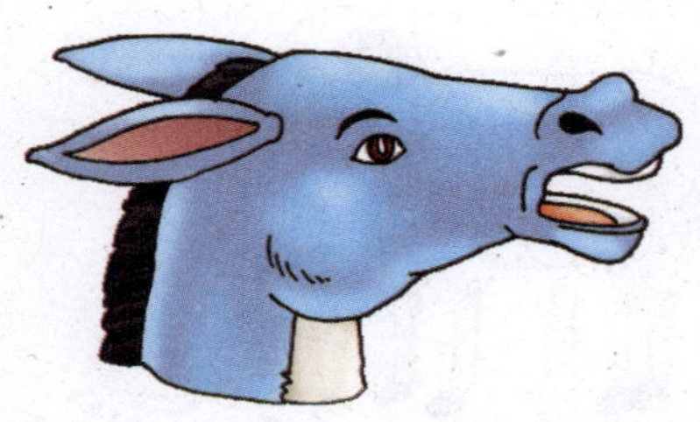

ass	bray	hyena	scream
ass	bray	hyena	scream
ass	bray	hyena	scream

monkey	chatter	bear	growl
monkey	chatter	bear	growl
monkey	chatter	bear	growl

Animal young ones

bird nestling | sheep lamb

bird nestling | sheep lamb

bird nestling | sheep lamb

dog puppy | hawk bowet

dog puppy | hawk bowet

dog puppy | hawk bowet

Male-Female

horse	mare	lad	lass
horse	mare	lad	lass
horse	mare	lad	lass

emperor	empress	man	woman
emperor	empress	man	woman
emperor	empress	man	woman

Antonyms

asleep	awake	land	water
asleep	awake	land	water
asleep	awake	land	water

day	night	top	bottom
day	night	top	bottom
day	night	top	bottom

Countries and Capitals

Italy Rome | England London

Italy Rome | England London

Italy Rome | England London

Greece Athens | India Delhi

Greece Athens | India Delhi

Greece Athens | India Delhi

microphone dynamite computer

microphone dynamite computer

microphone dynamite computer

photography phone satellite

photography phone satellite

photography phone satellite

Let us practice writing sentences. First trace and then try to write own.

The sun is a star. It is the

The sun is a star. It is the

source of light on earth. It rises

source of light on earth. It rises

in the east. It sets in the west.

in the east. It sets in the west.

Moon shines at night. Let us know about moon. First trace and then try to write own.

The moon shines at night. It has

The moon shines at night. It has

no light of its own. It refletcts

no light of its own. It refletcts

the light of the sun.

the light of the sun.

Its light is charming. The full

Its light is charming. The full

moon looks like a silver disc in

moon looks like a silver disc in

the sky. It is the natural

the sky. It is the natural

satellite of the earth.

satellite of the earth.

Let us know about the seasons. They are four in number. First trace and then try to write own.

We have four main seasons in

We have four main seasons in

our country. They are summer,

our country. They are summer,

rainy, spring and winter.

rainy, spring and winter.

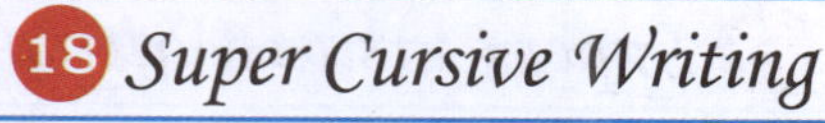

In summer, we receive a lot of

In summer, we receive a lot of

heat from the sun. All sources

heat from the sun. All sources

of water dry in this season.

of water dry in this season.

We feel a shortage of water.

We feel a shortage of water.

We sweat a lot in this season

We sweat a lot in this season

We get mangoes and other fruits

We get mangoes and other fruits

in this season. Holi is the

in this season. Holi is the

main festival of this season.

main festival of this season.

Rainy season is very important

Rainy season is very important

to us.

to us.

Farmers prepare their fields for

Farmers prepare their fields for

crops in this seaon. If there is

crops in this seaon. If there is

no rain, there is no food.

no rain, there is no food.

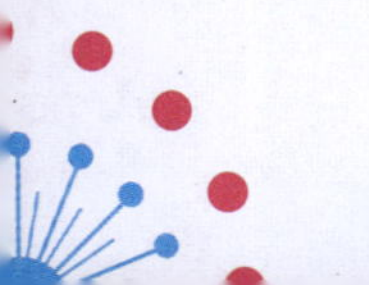

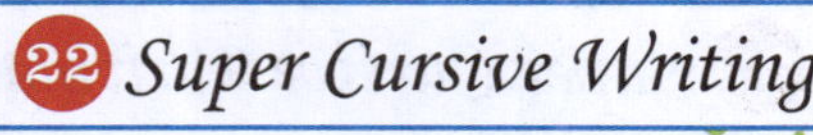

Let us know about a light ray. They are four in number. First trace and then try to write own.

The sunlight has seven colours.

The sunlight has seven colours.

But we cannot see them

But we cannot see them

normally. By using a prism,

normally. By using a prism,

we can see the colours. The

we can see the colours. The

colours are : violet, indigo, blue,

colours are : violet, indigo, blue,

green, yellow, orange and red.

green, yellow, orange and red.

Rainbow has these seven colours.

Rainbow has these seven colours.

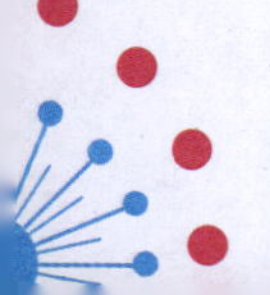

A rainbow can be seen before

A rainbow can be seen before

or after the rain. It looks very

or after the rain. It looks very

beautiful in the sky.

beautiful in the sky.

Let us know about English calendar. They are four in number. First trace and then try to write own.

Thirty days have September,

Thirty days have September,

April, June and Novermber.

April, June and Novermber.

All the rest have thirty one days.

All the rest have thirty one days.

Except February alone has

Except February alone has

twenty eight days. February of

twenty eight days. February of

a leap year has twenty nine days.

a leap year has twenty nine days.

Twelve months make a full

Twelve months make a full

year. A calendar is very useful

year. A calendar is very useful

thing. We can make our plans

thing. We can make our plans

with the help of a calendar.

with the help of a calendar.

Let us know about some important dates. They are four in number. First trace and then, try to write own.

1st January is celebrated as

1st January is celebrated as

the New year day. On 21st

the New year day. On 21st

March, day and night are equal.

March, day and night are equal.

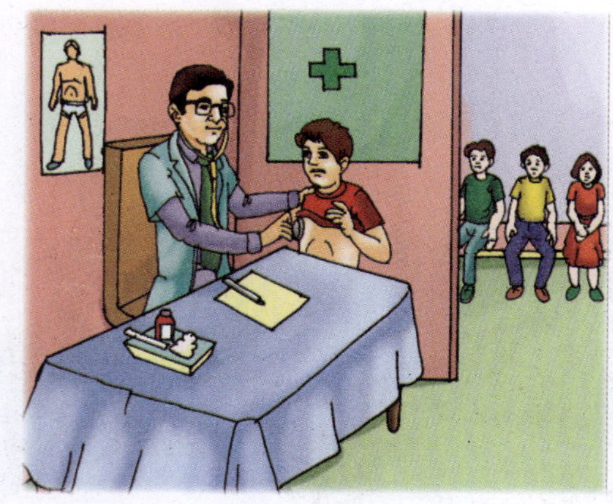

World health day is celebrated

World health day is celebrated

on 7th April. World No Tobacco

on 7th April. World No Tobacco

day is celebrated on 31st May.

day is celebrated on 31st May.

5th June is celebrated as

5th June is celebrated as

World Environment Day.

World Environment Day.

Childhood has no foreboding.

Childhood has no foreboding.

Childhood has no foreboding.

Childhood has no foreboding.

A boy's will is the wind's will.

A boy's will is the wind's will.

A boy's will is the wind's will.

A boy's will is the wind's will.

Read the Poem. Then trace and write.

I am bouncing, bouncing everywhere,
I bounce and bounce into the air;
I bounce and bounce then fall down.

I am bouncing, bouncing everywhere,
I bounce and bounce into the air;
I bounce and bounce then fall down.

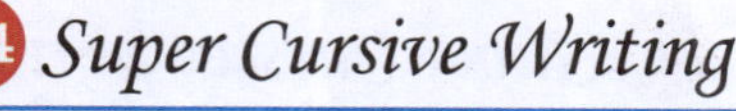

Read the Poem. Then trace and write.

Doctor Foster went to the Gloucester

in a shower of rain.

He stepped in, puddle,

Right up to his middle,

And never went there again.

Doctor Foster went to the Gloucester

in a shower of rain.

He stepped in . puddle,

Right up to his middle,

And never went there again.

Try to write about your favourite food by own.

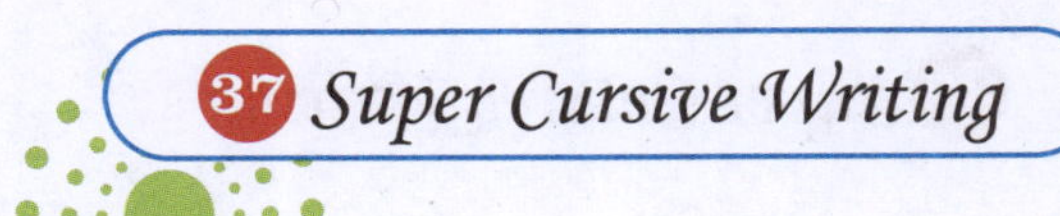

Try to write about your favourite festival.

Try to write about our country India.

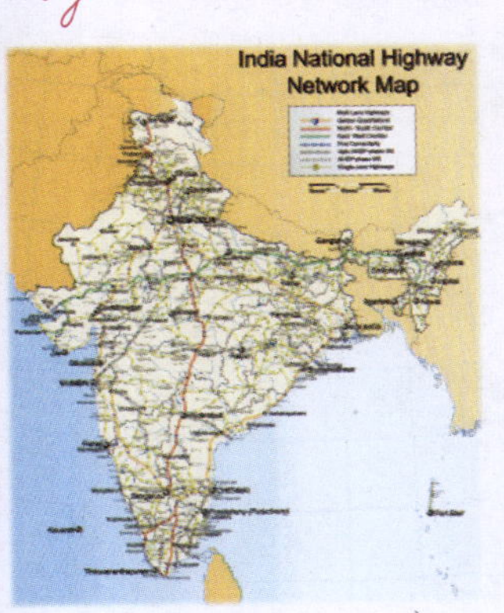

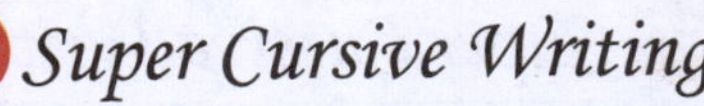

Paste the picture of your family in the box given below. Write a few lines about your family.